School Dress Codes

Other titles in the *Hot Pro/Con Issues* series

The Abortion Conflict
A Pro/Con Issue
ISBN 0-7660-1193-3

Animal
Experimentation
and Testing
A Pro/Con Issue
ISBN 0-7660-1191-7

The Death Penalty
for Teens
A Pro/Con Issue
ISBN 0-7660-1370-7

Drug
Legalization
A Pro/Con Issue
ISBN 0-7660-1197-6

Drug Testing
in Schools
A Pro/Con Issue
ISBN 0-7660-1367-7

Rain Forests
A Pro/Con Issue
ISBN 0-7660-1202-6

Separate Sexes,
Separate Schools
A Pro/Con Issue
ISBN 0-7660-1366-9

Space
Exploration
A Pro/Con Issue
ISNB 0-7660-1199-2

School Dress Codes

A Pro/Con Issue

Bárbara C. Cruz

Enslow Publishers, Inc.

40 Industrial Road   PO Box 38
Box 398   Aldershot
Berkeley Heights, NJ 07922   Hants GU12 6BP
USA   UK

http://www.enslow.com

Dedication

For my dear colleagues
Jimmy Duplass, Howard Johnston,
and Michael Berson,
who continue to positively influence
generations of educators.

Library of Congress Cataloging-in-Publication Data

Cruz, Bárbara C.
    School dress codes: a pro/con issue / Bárbara C. Cruz.
        p. cm. — (Hot pro/con issues)
    Includes bibliographical references and index.
    Summary: Examines the debate over whether or not to have
dress codes or uniforms in public schools.
    ISBN 0-7660-1465-7
    1. Dress codes—United States—Juvenile literature. [1. Dress codes.]
    I. Title. II. Series.
    LB3024 .C78 2000
    371.8—dc21

                                    00-021972

Printed in the United States of America

10 9 8 7 6 5 4 3 2

To Our Readers: We have done our best to make sure all Internet
addresses in this book were active and appropriate when we went to
press. However, the author and the publisher have no control over and
assume no liability for the material available on those Internet sites or on
other Web sites they may link to. Any comments or suggestions can be
sent by e-mail to comments@enslow.com or to the address on the back
cover.

Illustration Credits: AP/Wide World Photos, pp. 9, 15, 18, 37, 46,
53; Courtesy of EyeWire, Inc., p. 3; Skjold Photographs, p. 31.

Cover Illustration: Courtesy of EyeWire, Inc.

Contents

Chapter 1

The Controversy

Twelve-year-old Teshana Byars had already worn her blue jeans to school once. She had been warned that they were not allowed by the Waterbury, Connecticut, school system's dress code. The second time Teshana wore jeans to school, in March, 1999, she was sent to the principal's office. When the seventh grader refused to go, administrators called the police to arrest her for criminal trespass (entering the school illegally). Teshana's parents angrily said that the dress policy violated their parental rights and their daughter's constitutional rights (those privileges guaranteed to all citizens by the U.S. Constitution).

Dress codes were again at the center of controversy after the shooting tragedy at Columbine High School in Littleton, Colorado, on April 20, 1999. Two students had smuggled in homemade pipe bombs, two sawed-off shotguns, a semiautomatic rifle, and an assault pistol. They were able to conceal the weapons in their camouflage clothing, topped by black trench coats. Before they committed suicide, they killed twelve students and a teacher and wounded twenty-one others. One of the immediate effects was the banning of trench coats in schools throughout the United States. It was seen as a way of breaking up cliques and reducing the number of concealed weapons brought to school. Within a matter of weeks, schools across the nation also banned Marilyn Manson- and gothic-style clothing. The shock rock band Marilyn Manson is named for actress Marilyn Monroe and murderer Charles Manson. Band members often wear all-black clothes, white face makeup, black lipstick and nail polish, and black fishnet stockings.

Then, in May 1999, a fifteen-year-old in Conyers, Georgia, brought to school a revolver and a sawed-off rifle, which he had hidden in the legs of his baggy jeans. He wounded six of his fellow students. School dress codes were again debated across the United States. Some schools banned T-shirts featuring "gangsta-rap" musicians such as Wu-tang Clan and Tupac Shakur, saying that they promoted violence. After these school shooting tragedies, teachers and parents began to worry more about safety. Meanwhile, the National School Boards Association estimates that students bring about one hundred thirty-five thousand guns to school each day.[1]

Increasingly, school districts are beefing up student dress codes. Officials are concerned that very loose clothing can hide weapons and that certain styles and brands are associated with cults or gangs. Many parents and educators insist that orderly dress can lead to more orderly student behavior and, as a result, to more learning. Massachusetts governor William Weld spoke for many when he said, "Whether students are in first grade or eighth grade, they are all in school for the same reason—to learn. And too often clothes distract kids from this goal."[2]

For teenagers, dress codes might lessen fashion competition. Teens tend to dress like others in their group. The desire to wear the latest fashions even drives some students to skip school to earn money for trendy clothes.

Mixed Feelings

But people have mixed feelings about dress codes. Restrictive dress codes and school uniforms are opposed by many parents, students, and civil libertarians (those who believe in the greatest amount of freedom of action and thought with the least amount of interference by the government). They say that these restrictions violate individual freedoms guaranteed by the U.S. Constitution. These rights include freedom of expression, religion, and privacy.

*P*olice escort T. J. Solomon, the fifteen-year-old who opened fire on his classmates, into the county courthouse in Conyers, Georgia. It was later ruled that Solomon would be tried as an adult for the shootings.

Students who oppose dress codes say it is their right to dress as they wish. They also do not believe that dress codes eliminate status symbols, improve discipline, or increase academic achievement, as some claim. One eighteen-year-old student pointed out the absurdity of having to conform to dress codes at school: "We [eighteen-year-olds] can smoke and vote, but we can't wear what we want!"[3]

An even more restrictive measure is the adoption of school uniforms. While they used to be worn only in private schools, a 1998 study reported that 25 percent of public schools in the ten largest states either had already adopted school uniforms or were considering them.[4] And at least a dozen states now have laws allowing school districts to make students wear uniforms.

Supporters say school uniforms help erase obvious distinctions between poor and rich young people. Parent Elsa Rojas said, "I was tired of seeing my daughter cry after school because she didn't have Guess jeans or Levi's. I couldn't afford it."[5] High school freshman Chemiya Carter said pressure to conform to fashion could be intense. "If you aren't wearing Nautica, Tommy Hilfiger or Ralph Lauren," she said, "it's like you are less of a person."[6] If everyone wore a uniform, it might reduce fashion competition.

Teachers report that students have a more serious, studious attitude when they are in uniform. Proponents of school uniforms believe that students would be less distracted and better able to concentrate on their studies. The focus, they say, would shift from clothing to academics. Joe Clark, a former principal whose controversial techniques were the subject of the movie *Lean On Me*, believes that dress codes are crucial for restoring order and learning in schools. He says that many students "have Calvin Klein jeans on their behinds and nothing on their minds."[7]

Many school administrators also believe that

uniforms cut down on behavior problems. "The advantage of uniforms," said one educator, "is that young people tend to behave the way they are dressed."[8] A national survey of over five thousand public school principals showed that 70 percent of them believe uniforms would reduce school violence.[9]

Being able to easily identify students may also improve school safety. School officials point out that uniforms make it easier to spot those who belong on campus and those who do not. High school principal Amado Cruz said, "You have to distinguish where student rights stop and public safety takes over."[10]

Some school administrators even say that they would like to hold parents responsible for their children's obedience to a uniform policy. School superintendent Glenn Reynolds believes that parents of frequent violators should be charged with a crime. He said, "If the parent is continuing to [allow] that, we feel it's contributing to the delinquency of a child."[11]

But not everyone thinks school uniforms are a good thing. Those opposed to school uniforms present many of the same arguments as those who object to dress codes. In addition, some parents say dressing children in uniforms is too costly. It may go against their religion or culture. Also, opponents of uniforms do not believe that uniforms equalize status among students. They argue that students will still express their individuality and make their economic class known through other means.

Critics say that serious school problems cannot be erased by simply ordering students to wear uniforms. Many parents also object to uniform policies, saying that dress should not be dictated by the school. Some parents have complained that the parent–child relationship is hurt when families are required to buy specific clothing. The director of the Massachusetts American Civil Liberties Union (ACLU) said, "It is an issue of personal freedom. Such decisions should reside with students and their families."[12] When students were required to wear uniforms in Eagle Pass, Texas, 432 parents requested exemptions based on philosophical or religious grounds. Very few waivers (special permissions) were granted, and thirteen parents filed lawsuits based on constitutional grounds. The class action (group) lawsuit is now in federal court.[13]

The controversies have even affected the way teachers dress. In some schools, teachers are not allowed to wear blue jeans, T-shirts, leggings, sweatshirts, or sweatpants. In Denver, school board member Rita Montero suggested that dress codes for teachers be included in their contracts. Montero says that too many teachers are careless about their personal appearance and "dress for yard work, not school work." The answer, she says, is for teachers to have a dress code just as the students do, so that teachers can set an example and win respect. The nearby Colorado Springs school district adopted a dress code for teachers in 1997. They hope that "professional dress will bring more order, respect, and possibly more learning."[14]

Discipline for Dress Code Offenders

Across the country, punishments for students who do not comply with dress policies range from reprimands to detention, in-school suspension, or expulsion. Some schools loan clothes by the day to students who are out of uniform.

Several dress code cases have been heard by the U.S. Supreme Court, but the Court has not fully settled the matter. On the one hand, the Court has made it clear that students do have personal freedoms and a right to voice their opinion in school. On the other hand, schools also have the authority to enforce community standards of dress and to ensure school safety. Public schools have the right to ban clothing that is considered harmful, obscene, or disruptive to learning. How the terms "harmful," "obscene," and "disruptive" are defined is at the center of the debate.

Chapter 2

The Case for School Dress Codes

When Frank Mickens arrived at Boys and Girls High School in 1985, it was one of the most dangerous schools in the nation. Mickens had been selected to be the principal of the troubled school, located in Bedford-Stuyvesant, a section of Brooklyn, New York. The new principal soon instituted a strict student dress code. Students were told not to wear gold jewelry and expensive coats. Seniors had to wear shirts and ties. Within five years, the school's ranking on the list of the country's most dangerous schools fell dramatically. The school could boast that 70 percent of the senior class went on to college. Even the students eventually agreed that the dress code was a good thing. John Dean, a seventeen-year-old senior, said of the dress code, "It cuts down on violence around the school. Because you don't have kids looking at each other and saying, 'You got what I don't have, so I'm gonna rob you'."[1]

Stopping School Violence

Some schools enforce dress codes to stop school violence. As one educator put it, "We have dress codes for the same reason we have stop lights."[2] The National School Safety Center recommends that schools enforce a school dress code as one way to make schools safer.[3] Preventing students from smuggling weapons into school is of vital concern. It has been estimated that in as many as 90 percent of school violence events, the students involved carried weapons in their pockets or waistbands.[4] Although some urban schools have metal detectors, only 4 percent of all school districts in the United

*M*any schools now ban backpacks because of safety concerns. Police dogs were used to check student backpacks for drugs as well as for bombs after the Cheektowaga, New York, high school received a letter threatening violence.

What Some Schools Ban

✓ *"headgear"* (baseball caps, hair nets, bandannas, picks, combs)

✓ *footwear* (open-toed shoes, sandals, backless shoes, flip-flops, steel-toed or cowboy boots, Doc Martens, Timberland boots)

✓ *revealing clothing* (midriff-baring tops, tube tops, halter tops, see-through clothing, tank tops, muscle shirts, spaghetti straps, mini skirts, short-shorts, spandex, underwear worn as clothing)

✓ *oversized or sagging clothing* (untucked shirts, jackets, baggy pants)

✓ *grunge wear* (torn or frayed jeans, ripped clothing)

✓ *offensive T-shirts* (profane, obscene, racist, or sexually explicit messages or graphics; any writing or pictures related to alcohol, drugs, or violence)

✓ *jewelry* (large medallions, chains, spikes, gang-related jewelry, occult-related jewelry, earrings on males, removable gold teeth caps)

✓ *outerwear* (jackets, trench coats, gloves, or sunglasses inside school building)

✓ *brand-name clothing* (college and sports team logos, Disney characters, designers such as Tommy Hilfiger, designer athletic shoes)

✓ *military or camouflage apparel*

✓*extreme makeup* (powder-white gothic makeup, black lipstick, black nail polish)

✓*hair styles* (shaved heads, designs shaved into hair, braids, zigzag parts, mohawks, bleached hair, unnatural colors, colored hair extensions, beads, hair ornaments)

✓*facial hair* (mustaches, sideburns, goatees or other beards)

✓*visible tattoos and piercings* (other than pierced ears)

✓*backpacks, bookbags, or sports bags*

✓*electronics* (cellular phones, beepers, pagers, personal stereos)

States have the devices. One safety measure has been to ban backpacks or to allow only clear or mesh bookbags, so the contents can be easily seen. Many schools require students to tuck in their shirts so they cannot hide guns in the waistbands of their pants.

Some school districts are threatened by violence between rival gangs. Administrators and parents worry that students may become the victims of violence due to mistaken identity. Students may be mistaken for gang members if they accidentally wear a certain color or style. "It used to be that students only had to worry about putting together clothes that matched," former California governor Pete Wilson said. "Today, the wrong combination can get you killed."[5] In Los Angeles, a six-year-old girl was beaten to death when her attackers thought her red sweater showed she was connected with a local gang.

Experts on youth gangs say that a school dress code is one piece of the school safety puzzle. For example, new gang recruits are likely to be middle school students. According to experts, this is because middle school students are easily influenced by peer pressure and intimidation.[6] Banning all forms of street wear at school might discourage this type of gang activity.

Just owning certain types of stylish clothing can spark a violent attack. A fifteen-year-old Detroit boy was shot by someone who wanted his basketball

*P*resident Bill Clinton holds a Chicago Cubs jacket presented to him by Cubs star Sammy Sosa, left. These sports team jackets, called starter jackets, are popular among many young people. Some teens have even been killed for their jackets.

shoes. Jackets that display the name and emblem of popular sports teams, called starter jackets, have been at the center of teen homicides in several United States cities. In Chicago, police had to create a new crime category, starter jacket murders, because so many teens were killed for their jackets. In Newark, New Jersey, wearing leather bomber jackets has resulted in death for some teenagers. One writer who studied the issue stated, "The pressure to have the coolest shoes, hippest jeans, and phattest jackets has been known to drive more than one adolescent to beg, steal, borrow or—even kill."[7]

School officials say that dress codes are needed for safety as well as security reasons. Oversized coats, jackets, and backpacks pose a storage problem in cramped schools, where there is not enough space for so many bulky items. Loose clothing, open shoes, jewelry, and certain hairstyles can present safety problems in classes such as art, shop, or science labs.

Increasing Student Achievement

Many supporters of school dress codes say that the codes result in a more professional, businesslike atmosphere. Some schools call it "Dress for Success." They believe that dress codes can prepare young people for the "real world" of work. "I don't think a student should have to wear a shirt and tie to school every day," said William J. Saunders, executive director of the National Alliance of Black School Educators. "However, they should wear the same type of clothing one would wear to a job . . . with the main criterion being, 'What would you wear if you were going to work?'"[8]

Proponents also say that school dress codes may lead to higher academic achievement. Educators argue that dress codes are needed because the outlandish dress of some students can be distracting. Ian Halperin, spokesperson for the Mesquite, Texas, school district, said, "If you are looking at a guy with a purple mohawk and ten earrings, you probably aren't concentrating on your teacher as much as you should."[9]

Clothing that is too revealing is also considered distracting. Skirts or shorts that are too short, cropped tops, and spaghetti-strapped or sheer tops and dresses are banned in virtually every school district. Parent Cyndi Seibert said, "As the mother of a boy with teen-age hormones, [I think that] the uniform makes the young lady sitting next to him in biology lab less of a distraction, and the teacher a little easier to focus on, because she's got on a collared shirt with sleeves instead of a spaghetti strap with her bra hanging out."[10]

To help determine whether a student is dressed properly, many schools have adopted the "fingertip test." As a way of judging whether shorts or skirts are too short, students hold their arms to their sides. Only shorts and skirts that are longer than where the tips of the fingers reach are considered appropriate. Schools that want to be more precise use rulers and tape measures to determine acceptable length. In some schools, to judge whether a shirt or blouse is long enough, students are asked to lift their hands over their heads. If the bottom of the shirt rises above the waistband of their pants, it is unacceptable.

Many school districts are now considering dress codes for teachers. Most schools and districts request that teachers dress appropriately so they can serve as role models. The definition of "appropriate," however, is under debate. Some codes prohibit informal clothing such as shorts, T-shirts, and jeans. But some school districts are considering requiring male teachers to wear coats and ties and female teachers to wear skirts and stockings.

Teachers' unions are likely to oppose overly strict dress codes. The spokesperson for one educators' association warned that the rules on dress must be written jointly. "If [the rules] are heavy-handed," she said, "[the schools] are asking for trouble."[11]

One teenager believed that after a while, students would get used to dress codes. "We can still express ourselves and all of that. It doesn't bother anybody anymore, and it makes us look more presentable."[12]

Despite the many benefits that are claimed for school dress codes, however, many people still say they are unnecessary and maybe even illegal.

Chapter 3

The Case Against School Dress Codes

Jimmy Hines found himself in the national spotlight in 1991 when he and his parents decided to challenge the local school district's dress code. At issue was the gold-stud earring Jimmy wore in his left earlobe. Court cases challenging school dress codes usually use the First Amendment's guarantee of freedom of expression for support. Jimmy's case, however, involved the Ninth Amendment (which limits the power of government) and the Fourteenth Amendment (which offers equal protection to both sexes). Lawyers for the Hines family argued that since girls are allowed to wear earrings, not allowing boys to do so was a form of sex discrimination. Ultimately, the judge ruled in favor of Jimmy's Indiana school, citing community values and standards."[1]

Protests From Students and Parents

Although more schools are adopting stricter dress codes, students have not always been quick to accept them. At Bastrop High School in Austin, Texas, for example, two hundred students walked out of class and marched to school headquarters to protest a rule requiring students to tuck in their shirts. Officials explained that untucked shirts could conceal dangerous weapons. Students said that the rule was senseless, unfair, and violated their individualism. Protesting senior Alex Villaseñor explained, "They said we could conceal weapons with our shirt hanging out, but you could still take a weapon to school with a tucked-in shirt."[2] After hearings on the issue, the district decided that shirts made to be worn untucked would not have to be tucked in, as long as the bottom of the shirt was no longer than the place where the tips of the students' fingertips reached.

Not only students oppose dress codes. Many parents have also voiced their protests. In Mesquite, Texas, Rick Lannoye and his son, Mark, challenged the school dress code. Fifteen-year-old Mark was sent to the principal's office for wearing black clothes and a necklace with a silver star. School officials said the student's attire could be interpreted as gang-related. Rick Lannoye defended his son, saying that the black clothing and pentagram are symbols of Wicca, a nature-based pagan religion. Eventually, Mark was allowed to wear his necklace and all-black clothing. The experience prompted his father to propose a change to the dress code that would allow clothing that reflects religion, race, culture, or sexual orientation.

In Mississippi, the Harrison County School Board upheld a high school principal's decision not to allow a Jewish student to wear a Star of David pendant. Junior Ryan Green arrived on the first day of the 1999–2000 school year wearing the necklace, a gift from his Jewish grandmother. He was soon told either to wear it under his shirt or to take it off. School administrators believed that the pendant looked like a gang symbol. Even after protests and explanations from Ryan's father, the school board supported the principal's position. But after the controversial vote drew national attention, the school board reversed its ruling and allowed Ryan to wear the pendant.

Tinker v. *Des Moines Independent Community School District* is the landmark case in students' rights and school dress codes. Mary Beth Tinker and two other students were sent home from school in 1965 for wearing black armbands in protest against the Vietnam War. The Tinkers sued, arguing that the First Amendment of the U.S. Constitution protected the students' right to express their political views in a nondisruptive way. In 1969 the U.S. Supreme Court agreed, saying that as long as they do not disrupt the school environment, children do not leave their constitutional rights at the schoolhouse door. Since then, many suits have used *Tinker* as a precedent for challenging school dress codes.

The conflict between parental rights and school rights is part of the controversy. Thirteen-year-old Francisco Gamboa said, "The only people who should tell kids what to wear are their parents—not the school board, community, teachers, or principals. They don't have the right to do that."[3]

Thirteen-year-old Ben Sharpe's parents were enraged when they found out that their honors student son would not be able to speak at his eighth-grade graduation. Because the Sacramento, California, student had maintained a straight-A record, he was to receive the Superintendent's Award for excellence. In preparation, Ben's mother took him to the barber. Since it was summer, she asked that his hair be cut very short. On the day of the ceremony the Sharpes were shocked when Ben was not allowed to participate because his haircut did not conform to the school's dress code. Ben's father, Frank Sharpe, expressed his anger to school officials: "I told them that they have no right to rob my son of what he rightfully earned."[4]

Hair braids have been particularly controversial. When African-American third grader Megan Smith was sent home from school because she wore thick braids, her parents were furious. "There's a cultural difference there," they said. "You're penalizing us for having a different type of hair."[5]

Dress Codes Discriminate

Some ethnic minorities have felt that certain dress codes are racially discriminatory. The National Association for the Advancement of Colored People (NAACP) chapter in Thomasville, Georgia, got involved in the high school dress code issue when students were prohibited from displaying Malcolm X symbols or messages. Because the code banned any racial slurs or slogans, it also prohibited any race-specific messages. When students wore T-shirts with messages such as "The Blacker the college, the sweeter the knowledge," they received warnings from the school administration. The NAACP argued that the code was unfairly aimed at African-American students.

Graduation ceremonies have sparked several bitter disputes. Schools tend to have strict dress codes regarding what students may and may not

What Are Students' Legal Rights Regarding Dress?

Although the courts have established that students do have the right of freedom of expression, they have also ruled that the right is in relation to the need for a positive learning environment. Here are the most famous court cases regarding students and school dress codes:

Tinker v. Des Moines Independent School District (1969) This landmark U.S. Supreme Court case upheld students' right to make a political statement at school. When Mary Beth Tinker wore a black armband to school in protest against the Vietnam War, the Court affirmed students' right to do so.

Scott v. Board of Education, Union Free School District #17 (1969) When girls were prohibited from wearing pants to school, the Supreme Court of New York did not support the district's dress code. Because neither safety nor discipline were jeopardized, the court ruled the dress policy violated the female students' rights.

Davenport v. Randolph County Board of Education (1984) Athletes may be subject to dress code policies beyond the general code for the school. The Eleventh Circuit Court upheld a high school's "clean shaven" policy for football and basketball team players.

Olesen v. Board of Education of School District No. 228 (1987) A district court in Illinois agreed that a school board may adopt a general rule of prohibiting the wearing of any gang symbols. When a high school boy argued that his rights were violated when he was not allowed to wear an earring, the court dismissed his claim and upheld the dress code intended to discourage gangs.

Harper v. Edgewood Board of Education (1987) An Ohio district court agreed that school dress code policies are related to community values. It upheld a high school's prohibition of a brother and sister attending the prom dressed in clothes of the opposite sex.

Broussard v. School Board of City of Norfolk (1992) Although the antidrug message on a student's T-shirt was positive, one of the words was considered vulgar. The school's dress code was upheld by a U.S. district court in Virginia.

Jeglin* v. *San Jacinto Unified School District (1993) If a high school can prove that certain sports logos are affiliated with gangs, students may be prohibited from wearing clothing with those insignias. The ban at the high school level in this case was upheld by a U.S. district court in California. But it was found to be unconstitutional at the elementary and middle school levels because there was insufficient proof of gang activity at those levels.

Pyle* v. *South Hadley School Committee (1993) The two Pyle brothers were disciplined for wearing T-shirts to their high school that administrators found vulgar even though one of the messages was antialcohol. A district court in Massachusetts upheld the school's right to prohibit the T-shirts, agreeing that the shirts were at odds with the district's educational mission.

Barber* v. *Colorado Independent School District (1995) The Texas Supreme Court upheld community standards and ruled that although eighteen-year-old high school students have reached the age of majority, they do not have the same constitutional rights as adults. As such, an eighteen-year-old male high school student was prohibited from wearing earrings and long hair to school.

Hines* v. *Caston School Corporation (1995) The Indiana Court of Appeals upheld a prior judgment supporting a school's dress code policy of not allowing male students to wear earrings to school. Citing the "community standards of dress," only girls are allowed to wear the jewelry in school.

Bivens by and through Green* v. *Albuquerque Public Schools (1995) When a student continued to wear sagging pants after several warnings, he was suspended from school. The U.S. District Court of New Mexico found that the style was not a form of protected speech and that the school had the right to prohibit gang-related clothing.

Phoenix Elementary School District No. 1* v. *Green (1995) When two students attended school wearing T-shirts to protest the no-opt-out uniform policy, they were expelled. A court of appeals in Arizona upheld the school district's policy, which tried to stop gang activity and reduce fashion competition.

wear. Some even define what clothes may be worn under students' graduation gowns.

When she was a student at Oak Park–River Forest High School in Chicago, Genevieve York-Erwin's hard work paid off when she became valedictorian of her 1998 graduating class. At her school, the hundred-year-old dress code for graduation required girls to wear long white dresses and carry a dozen red roses. Boys traditionally wore dark suits, white shirts, and red ties.

Eighteen-year-old Genevieve said she did not like dresses and did not even own one. She said that she was certainly not going to wear one for graduation. She also felt the dress code was sexist, because while the boys could wear their suits later at job interviews, the girls would be able to wear their impractical dresses only at formal events. School officials stated that Genevieve would not be able to attend the event or deliver her speech before her six hundred classmates. She offered to wear a dressy white pantsuit instead, but the school administration said the rules could not be changed.

Students were divided over the issue. Some supported the dress code, saying that the tradition linked the more than fifty-five thousand graduates who had participated in it. Others agreed that the code was old-fashioned. Genevieve and another student began a petition. They collected more than a thousand signatures from students, teachers, and parents supporting Genevieve's position. Her mother, Nancy York-Erwin, applauded her daughter's decision—even if it meant that Genevieve would have to miss the ceremony.

Ultimately, the valedictorian was not allowed to participate in the ceremony. Genevieve sat in the audience watching her classmates. She later received her diploma in the principal's office. Her mother was on hand to snap some photographs of the event. Genevieve said, "I will go away from my high school experience somewhat bitter toward this place that has been otherwise wonderful." She entered Yale University the following fall and continued to believe she had done the right thing.[6]

At a high school in Denver, Colorado, seniors Aisha Price and Enockina Ocansey wanted to wear bright kente cloth sashes with their white graduation gowns. Kente cloth is a richly colored fabric, originally from Ghana, Africa. Many African Americans wear it as a symbol of ethnic pride. The sashes were handwoven with the words "Arvada High School Class of 1998." The African-American girls saw them as a symbol of pride and diversity. School officials prohibited the girls from wearing the sashes, saying that there was a need to "preserve the unity of the graduation ceremony."[7] Officials were also concerned that if the sashes were allowed, it would open the door for other garb, some of which might be offensive. Ultimately, the school's decision was upheld in federal court. As a concession, the students were allowed to wear their sashes during Senior Week activities.

Gender and athletic dress codes were the issues in 1995 when the Gulliver Prep High School's track team placed third in a state meet. The all-girl team was disqualified, however, because of their high-cut running briefs. Coach Karen Callaway complained to race officials, explaining that several of the girls wore the short shorts because they cut down on wind drag. She also pointed out that Olympic and college athletes wore these shorts.

The Florida High School Activities Association (FHSAA) upheld the race officials' decision, much to the dismay of the coach, the girls, and their parents. When the team appealed the decision at the national level, the National Federation of State High School Athletic Associations said that individual states were free to interpret the rule. Critics felt that the FHSAA was being gender-biased. That is, it did not take girls as seriously as boys in athletics. After all, they argued, the girls just wanted a competitive edge.

Guidelines Are Unclear

One of the problems has been the vague wording of some school policies. In many schools and districts where such measures have been adopted, the guidelines have been unclear, mentioning only that "professional attire" is required. This frustrates many parents, who believe that too much in the codes is left up to school officials' interpretation. Parent Sherrie Ellis believes that her daughter's school rule against wearing "anything that's offensive to administrators or personnel" is too vague and that administrators need to be more specific. "What *can* our children wear?" she asked.[8]

Some students challenge the dress code by complying with the letter of the law, but not with its spirit. At Rockhurst School in Kansas City, for example, all shirts are required to have collars, so some students wear flowery Hawaiian shirts or bowling shirts. One Rockhurst student said, "If I'm going to be forced to wear clothes for a dress code, I'm going to be as close to non–dress code policies as possible." Another student at a nearby school agreed, saying, "I like the challenge of finding out what I can and can't get away with."[9]

Some believe that imposing arbitrary rules such as dress codes may cause teenagers to become more rebellious. In the end, they argue, strict dress codes may actually alienate students. Dave Skillman, a St. Louis high school principal, said, "I think clothing choices are just that, choices. I think it's very important to teenagers, and if it's not distracting or offensive to others, I think that's an area where choice is important."[10] Nicole Harrow, thirteen years old, agreed, saying, "I think as long as you dress civilly and you're not walking around in a bathing suit or something, it doesn't matter what you wear. I mean, if you wear shirts with curses on it or something, I can see why they say not to. But if you dress nicely and you're not offending anybody, it's OK."[11]

*S*ome students have found creative ways of complying with their school's dress codes. At one school that required all shirts to have collars, some students wore flowery Hawaiian shirts like this one.

Some people are alarmed by any kind of dress code. One ACLU official says that if a student's clothing "does not disrupt the educational process or constitute a threat to safety, it should be of no concern to the school."[12] Some people are also concerned that looking different from others might be automatically seen as a problem. An ACLU lawyer, Ann Beeson, said, "There seems to be an effort now to target any kid who dresses differently;

schools are equating being different with being dangerous."[13] Fifteen-year-old Patrick Connor feels that wearing his metal-studded jacket should not be taken as a sign that he is violent. "Just because we have chains and spikes," he said, "doesn't mean we're going to go shooting people."[14]

One young adult elegantly summarized the position against school dress codes this way:

> Clothes symbolize who a person is as an individual and I do not feel that there should be dress codes enforced in schools or any other public facility. This is America and we have a choice to express ourselves in any fashion which we feel comfortable portraying as long as it does not violate any laws. Clothing makes us different and unique and more aware of the diverse cultures within our nation. Dress codes seem to eliminate this awareness.[15]

Chapter 4

The Case for School Uniforms

For many people, school uniforms create the image of orderly, safe schools that emphasize academics. Traditionally, uniforms have been associated primarily with private schools. But today thousands of public schools have begun to require that students wear uniforms. These are mostly elementary and middle schools, but some high schools are included, too. Mike Casserly is the executive director of the Council of the Great City Schools, an association of the nation's fifty largest school districts. According to him, at the beginning of the 1997–1998 school year, more than half of the urban school districts in the United States had a uniform policy.[1] Growing numbers of schools in cities like Baltimore, Boston, Cleveland, Chicago, Detroit, Los Angeles, Miami, New Orleans, New York, San Antonio, and Seattle are requiring students to attend school in uniform.

Uniforms Promote Better Student Behavior

Supporters of school uniforms believe that dress codes do not go far enough. They say that student attitudes and behavior would be improved if all students were required to wear uniforms. Supporters have many reasons for wanting students to wear uniforms: school safety, stronger focus on academics, better student conduct and attendance, school pride, reduced competition, less peer pressure and racial tension. The measure got strong support at a national conference on school violence in October 1998. There, the nation's mayors called for the widespread mandatory adoption of school uniforms. Twelve-year-old Marcus Sheffield said, "I like wearing uniforms. It's safer. We don't have to worry about somebody trying to steal our clothes. And it also forces us to concentrate more on our school work than on what everybody else is wearing."[2]

When fifty-five hundred public school principals were surveyed in 1996, 70 percent of them said they believed uniforms cut down on discipline problems.[3] A 1998 survey by the Council of the Great City Schools found that uniform policies were a growing trend.

The first voluntary uniform policy in a public school was started in Baltimore's Cherry Hill Elementary in 1987. Originally, the policy was begun in response to increasing school violence and gangs. Today, almost all students wear uniforms. A spokesperson for the school district said that students loved wearing their uniforms. "They have this mentality from seeing private school kids," she said. "Everyone feels equal and important."[4]

Will Uniforms Make Schools Better or Worse?

Do you think requiring students to wear uniforms to school will make our public schools better, worse, or make no difference?

✓ better 52%

✓ worse 14%

✓ no difference 34%

Source: Marist Institute of Public Opinion, Marist College, telephone poll conducted on August 27, 1996.

School uniforms are favored by many prominent politicians. President Bill Clinton has often said that school uniforms can provide a sense of identity and self-worth and can eliminate dress as a status symbol. In his January 1996 State of the Union address he encouraged public schools to consider adopting school uniforms as a way to promote order and teach young people good citizenship. He then directed the Department of Education to send a policy manual on school uniforms to every district in the nation. In his memo to the Secretary of Education, President Clinton identified uniforms as part of an overall program to improve school safety and discipline. He wrote, "Too often, we learn that students resort to violence and theft simply to obtain designer clothes or fancy sneakers. Too often, we learn that clothing items worn at school, bearing special colors or insignias, are used to identify gang membership or instill fear among students and teachers alike."[5]

Clinton's enthusiasm was due in large part to the reports from Long Beach, California, the first public school district to require uniforms in elementary and middle schools, in 1994. Parents had been concerned that their children might be attacked by gangs for wearing the wrong color by mistake. Within the first four years of the new policy, officials reported a 91 percent drop in school crime, a 92 percent decrease in weapons offenses, and a 62 percent reduction in drug charges. The district also reported higher test scores, and attendance reached an all-time high. At the city's high school, where uniforms were not required, no similar improvements were recorded.

Enthusiastic reports such as these encouraged other school districts to consider both voluntary and mandatory uniform policies. In Miami, Florida, Demetrio Pérez, Jr., described uniforms as "the most critical issue" among the twenty-five initiatives he proposed during his bid for a seat on the school board. Apparently, voters agreed, because Pérez won and became the school board vice chairman.

Uniforms Promote Better Grades

Supporters say that uniforms may improve academic performance because they promote a more scholarly environment. More formal clothing puts students in the right mind-set to learn. Teachers say that since the learning climate is improved, they can focus more on teaching and less on discipline problems. Principal Pamela Hoffler Riddick said that

*S*tudents at Amosland Elementary School in Philadelphia began wearing uniforms in 1999. Across Pennsylvania, many schools are adopting uniforms in an attempt to improve discipline and school security.

when students wear uniforms, "The focus is moved from the neck down to the neck up."[6]

Uniforms Promote School Spirit

Uniforms may also promote school spirit. In some schools, uniform pride has developed, as students feel their uniforms set them apart from other schools. One principal in Kansas City, Missouri, said that in her school, "The children feel good about themselves as school uniforms build a sense of pride."[7] In New York City, where the school board unanimously approved mandatory uniforms in elementary schools, school board spokesman Philip

Russo said in 1997 that the program was a success: "Even kids who initially don't like the idea say they feel they're being treated with more respect. It really breeds a lot of unity and self-esteem."[8] New York mayor Rudy Giuliani enthusiastically supported the Board of Education's decision. He said, "I've always believed that school uniforms are one important part of creating an environment in which students respect themselves, respect one another, and respect their schools as hallowed places of learning."[9]

Away from school, a group of students in uniform tend to be regarded positively by the public. A school security expert said, "To many in the community, a school uniform is a symbol of education, projecting a positive rather than negative image."[10] School principal Roger Harris agreed, saying, "It changes the perception people have of our students on the streets. They're seen as students, not gang members."[11]

Many parents and teachers believe that uniforms promote better student behavior. Pam Dukes, a parent who was pleased when her child's school adopted uniforms, said, "Our theory is when a child is dressed nice, he acts better."[12] Evidence from some school districts seems to support this. One principal in Louisville, Kentucky, said that on "out of uniform days," when students are allowed to wear street clothes, "the behavior and attitude is as different as night and day."[13]

One year after instituting a mandatory uniform policy at South Shore Middle School in Seattle, Washington, principal John German said that student attitudes and behavior had improved 98 percent. After the policy took effect, he noticed that students were more academically focused.

Many Students Prefer Uniforms

Perhaps most surprising is that many students, older ones included, actually seem to prefer school uniforms. Lloyd Choice, principal of Jack Yates High School in Houston, was shocked when students started lobbying for uniforms. "Pretty soon the parents caught on," Choice said. "On opening day this fall, I tell you, it just brought tears to your eyes. Out of 1,800 kids, we had 12 report not in uniform." After thirty-five years in the public schools, Choice said, "I didn't believe it would affect behavior, but it does. My children are behaving so much better. I had to experience it to believe it."[14]

After the San Antonio Independent School District began requiring uniforms in some schools, Associate Superintendent David Splitek enthusiastically reported fewer disruptions than ever before. The following year all ninety-four schools instituted a uniform policy. At first, students resisted the new rule, but soon many of them began to favor it. Dwain Smith, a seventeen-year-old senior, said, "Last year we were all against it, but now that we're into it, I kind of like it because it's easier. You just get your uniform together and go."[15]

Uniforms Save Parents Money

Some parents like the convenience and low cost of uniforms. They insist that in the long run, uniforms save money. They argue that a week's worth of uniforms costs much less than the trendy, name-brand outfits favored by most students. And while certain clothing styles go out of fashion, the uniforms stay the same. Uniforms made out of durable material can be passed on from one sibling to another.

Parents also like the fact that most school uniforms are easy to launder and do not need ironing.

One of the attractions of a uniform policy is that it may blur differences in economic class. If everyone dresses alike, the distinction between the haves and the have-nots is less apparent. Uniforms may reduce the teasing of students who cannot afford to dress in the trendiest styles. "With uniforms," said a spokesperson for schools in Long Beach, California, "no one can say 'Your mother dresses you funny' 'cause they're wearing the exact same thing."[16] Many students like uniforms because they make everyone seem more equal in terms of economic status. Middle schooler Jackie Ríos said, "Having uniforms is a lot better, because people cannot talk about and laugh at your clothes."[17]

Parents also point out that uniforms end morning arguments over clothes. Principal and mother Nora Rosensweig said, "From a parent's standpoint, I'd love it for my own child because I get tired of arguing about what to wear every morning."[18] Many students admit that it is easier to choose what to wear in the morning. Sixteen-year-old Colin Stewart said, "Sometimes uniforms can be a pain, but they do take a lot of pressure off of fashion decisions."[19] George Berganza, fourteen, agreed: "With uniforms, you don't have to think about competition. You don't have to think about labels or if you're wearing something too often."[20]

Supporters insist that uniforms do not eliminate individuality. When President Bill Clinton visited Long Beach, California, he spoke to the students and teachers at Jackie Robinson Academy. Uniforms, he said, "slowly teach our young people one of life's most important lessons: that what really counts is what you are and what you can become on the inside, not what you are wearing on the outside."[21]

Students say that despite having to wear uniforms, they can express their individuality in other ways. One sixteen-year-old student said, "I attend an all-girls Catholic high school, and even though we have uniforms, we're still able to express ourselves by the shoes we wear, our hairstyles, and other accessories."[22] Parent Paula Dodd agreed: "Individuality shouldn't come from their clothing but from a spirit within."[23]

Chapter 5

The Case Against School Uniforms

When Lawrence High School in Massachusetts began requiring school uniforms, students who did not wear them faced detention. One student, Crystal Duquette, was suspended three times during her senior year for not wearing the uniform and not serving detention. The protest she and her parents waged resulted in the policy being dropped the following year. Later, as a college student, Crystal said, "I'm proud to say I never wore my uniform. It wasn't going to help me learn any better."[1]

Uniforms Do Not Fix School Problems

Many educators and students do not think that uniforms result in a stronger academic focus. "Don't think that by forcing students to wear uniforms you're going to get them to concentrate more on their studies," said Sybil Renick. Her school required uniforms but allowed students to select their own shoes. She recalls, "We spent just as much time talking about each other's shoes as we did listening to our teachers."[2]

Opponents of uniforms have called them a "Band-Aid approach" to solving serious school problems. Rather than treating causes, they say, uniforms merely address the symptoms. They argue that any improvements that occur as a result of students wearing uniforms are likely to be temporary. Uniforms do not get at the root of much-needed educational reform.

Many educators point out that something as simple as clothing cannot correct serious problems. High school headmaster William Wassell said, "I honestly don't feel the wearing of uniforms will enhance the atmosphere in a school. A lot of other factors determine the atmosphere and environment that exists in a school."[3] LaKnogony McCurley, a

Should Public Schools Require Uniforms?

Would you favor or oppose allowing your school district to require students in public schools to wear uniforms?

✓ favor 52%

✓ oppose 43%

✓ do not know 5%

Source: New York Times/CBS News, telephone poll conducted on April 2, 1996.

high school junior, agreed. She said that uniforms would not transform anyone into a good student, just "dress up a bad one."[4]

Some critics say that the complex problem of gangs cannot be easily fixed by school uniforms. They say that the causes of gang violence—including poverty, lack of family involvement, and the lack of positive role models—must be addressed. They also point out that school uniforms might actually make it easier for gang members to slip unnoticed into schools. Without the easily recognizable clothing of gangs, teachers and administrators would not be able to distinguish gang members from other students.

Many people say that requiring either strict dress codes or uniforms is a political ploy. Since these policies do not involve raising taxes, critics say, politicians may support them as an easy fix for a complex problem. Critics maintain that the focus should be on more important issues. Marc Posner of the Education Development Center in Boston said, "For politicians, it's a lot easier to endorse [uniforms] because they don't cost [the government] anything—than find the resources to hire more teachers, improve the student–teacher ratio and repair facilities."[5] Thirteen-year-old Nicole Harrow agreed: "I think that they're so busy worrying about school uniforms, they don't think about the main problems that kids have in school, like drugs and gangs. How to get money to fund programs in school and get books that are new."[6]

Opponents of school uniforms say that although wearing uniforms is seen as an obvious and concrete means of bringing order and discipline to the classroom, there is no solid evidence that they actually reduce violence. Many parents and educators doubt that uniforms decrease misbehavior, because there is little data on the cause-and-effect relationship between uniforms and violence. While uniform policies may indirectly affect a school's environment by serving as a symbol of commitment, uniform policies are usually started along with other policy changes, such as increasing the number of adults patrolling hallways during class changes or having a clearer discipline code. So critics say it is difficult to determine which policy change has resulted in improved behavior. Nadine Strossen, president of the ACLU, says, "Throughout society, there is popular support for any measure that sounds like it supports greater law and order, even if there's no evidence that it actually has any effect."[7]

Another explanation for the immediate success of school uniforms may be what researchers call the Hawthorne Effect. Because uniforms may be seen as new and special, students may behave differently because of the novelty. After the new policy has been in place for some time, warn critics, behavior may return to that of preuniform days. As seventh grader Josh Taitano pointed out, "You can get in just as much trouble with your uniform on."[8]

Often a school district adopts a uniform policy only for the elementary grades. Some people say this makes no sense, since discipline problems and serious violence are more common in high schools. Yet, according to the U.S. Department of Education, only about one percent of United States high schools require uniforms.

Younger children may be less inclined to express themselves through their clothing and more willing to wear uniforms, but high school students are more likely to resist uniforms. Rachel Vanderford, a high school senior, explained, "From the ages of 14 to 18 you're trying to find your identity, and I think it's a lot harder to find your identity when you look like everybody else."[9]

Uniforms Inhibit Individuality

Opponents argue that uniforms stress conformity at a time when schools are supposedly trying to help students understand and accept diversity in our society. One San Diego student complained,

*O*ne of the complaints against school uniforms is that they can be a financial burden for families. Some people have complained that the uniforms schools loan to poor children are shabby and do not fit. This student is trying on a new uniform that is being altered to fit her properly.

"Teachers say they want us to be different, and then we all have to dress the same way."[10]

Some opponents also claim that by being required to wear uniforms, students are deprived of an important opportunity to make choices and set limits for themselves. This, in turn, would allow students to develop self-discipline. Sociologist Ruth Rubenstein is opposed to school uniforms because she feels that allowing young people to choose their own clothes prepares them for adulthood.[11] Most psychologists say that it is normal for teens to use fashion as a way of rebelling. They also say that the way adolescents dress does not always predict their behavior.[12]

Many teens say that uniforms do not equalize status in their schools—they still know who is rich and who is poor. At Notre Dame Academy in Kansas City, where school uniforms are required, students still find ways to discriminate. One senior said, "Just by looking at someone [in the uniform], you can tell who they are by their jewelry, makeup, hair." Another student, a sophomore at nearby St. Teresa's Academy, said, "What's on the inside is eventually going to discover a way to crawl through restrictions, creating and modifying a person's individual self on the outside. In a school that requires uniforms, self-expression is important and necessary and should be encouraged."[13]

Uniforms may also inhibit individuality and infringe upon personal freedom of speech. Ty Bowers, director of a clothing company, warned, "When you try and make people conform in one area, they make up for it somewhere else."[14] Besides, the ACLU concluded, "Ban every form of individual expression and what you have left are not students, but soldiers."[15]

It is against the law for public schools to require uniforms without allowing for exceptions based on religious or financial reasons. Most districts have an "opt-out" policy that allows families to ask for an exemption. But in 1995 an Arizona judge upheld a school uniform policy with a no opt-out condition.

Uniforms Are a Financial Burden

The ACLU has argued that many parents cannot afford to buy school uniforms. Especially in poor communities, a mandatory policy imposes an unfair financial burden on families. Hope Carradine, a parent with three school-age children, said she had to ask other relatives to help pay for the uniforms. "I shop thrift and buy in bulk," she explained. "You can't do that with uniforms."[16] One frustrated parent wrote a letter to the editor of her local newspaper, saying that the uniforms required by her daughter's school actually cost more than her school clothes in previous years. She wrote, "I initially spent $200 on uniforms and have since spent an additional $75 as the seasons changed, plus $20 spent on alterations. When I add these costs to the cost of 'regular clothing' for activities outside of the school day, I have actually spent more on my daughter's wardrobe this year than in years past. All of this money was spent to provide two separate wardrobes—one of which she doesn't even like."[17]

Soon after the Long Beach, California, school district started its mandatory uniform policy, the ACLU filed a lawsuit on behalf of twenty-six low-income families. Within a year, the parties reached an agreement. District officials loaned $180,000 worth of uniforms to needy students.

But merely providing loaned uniforms to students does not always solve the controversy. In Polk County, Florida, over five hundred parents and children signed on to the class action lawsuit filed against the school board. The county drew national attention when it became the nation's first school district to adopt a districtwide mandatory school uniform policy. One of the complaints listed in the lawsuit was that needy students were given shabby uniforms, marked with an "L," that did not always fit. The lawsuit also claimed that students faced suspension from school if they were not dressed in uniform.

The biggest criticism against uniforms is that it is unlawful to deprive students of an education simply because they do not follow a uniform policy. "What do you do if a student violates it?" asks high school principal Stephen Sangster. "Deny him an education?"[18] Loren Siegel of the ACLU said, "Every child in this country has the right to a public school education, and that right cannot be [based] upon compliance with a uniform policy."[19]

Chapter 6

The Bottom Line

Although the majority of United States schools do not require uniforms, almost all have some sort of dress code. The trend is toward strict codes. Increasingly, educators and parents believe that while mandatory school dress codes and uniforms may not be right for all school districts, they may be effective and appropriate in some settings.

There have been many legal challenges to dress codes. While the courts have not settled the issue completely, they have provided some direction. In the United States, the right of nonverbal self-expression has been upheld by the Supreme Court. Alan Howard, a professor of constitutional law, says that while schools can prohibit clothing considered disruptive or vulgar, they cannot ban clothes that simply express an unpopular opinion. If a student wears a T-shirt that says "Legalize Hemp," Howard said, "I would think the school would be hard-pressed to win that."[1]

Courts Uphold Dress Codes

Overall, courts have upheld dress codes when schools have been able to show that they were linked to the learning environment or to popular community standards. Students' dress can also be regulated by school officials for health and safety reasons. The trend in the courts has been to allow communities that feel they might benefit from school dress codes and uniforms to try them.

The courts have been most supportive of limitations on types of clothing allowed. Requiring students to dress in a particular way has been judged necessary to carry out the educational goal of schools. For the most part, dress codes have not been found to violate personal liberty, since clothing can be changed after school. Limitations on hair length and facial hair (such as sideburns, mustaches, and beards) have been more problematic. Since that requirement would affect students after the school day, rules regarding hair have been more difficult to uphold.

For schools that wish to have a dress code, experienced educators recommend that dress codes be clearly written, specific, and understandable by all. For example, in Phoenix, Arizona, a controversy regarding school dress codes began when parents complained that students were wearing revealing clothing. Eventually discussions resulted in a code that banned not only revealing clothing, but also T-shirts that were too bare or that had Disney characters. Security guards at Central High School were put on "T-shirt patrol." They asked students who wore improper clothing to turn their shirts inside out or sent them home. After complaints from some students and parents, the school district made a new code with clearer wording.[2]

One compromise is having dress-down days. Some schools require dress codes Monday through

Pros and Cons
of School Uniforms

Pros

Although research data have not firmly established a cause-and-effect relationship between school uniforms and student behavior, there are positive effects that have been documented:

- ✓ more of a focus on academics, less on clothing
- ✓ a decrease in verbal abuse among students
- ✓ a greater ability to identify people who do not belong in the school
- ✓ increased school pride

Cons

Critics of school uniforms believe that the policies:

- ✓ emphasize obeying rules over thinking for oneself
- ✓ unfairly punish all students for the deeds of a few
- ✓ are disrespectful of the right to freedom of expression
- ✓ emphasize sameness at a time when schools are trying to celebrate diversity

Source: Families Plus, "Adolescents and Clothes," n.d., <http://www.parenting-qa.com> (February 8, 2000).

*C*areful planning is needed to ensure a successful dress code or school uniform policy. The dress code at Harrison Middle School in Albuquerque is simple—students must wear either black or white clothing.

Thursday, but allow a free dress or casual day on Friday, when students may wear regular street clothes to school. Other schools allow dress-down days only once in a while.

Uniform Policies Require Careful Planning

For those schools considering uniforms, the ACLU warns that special funds should be set aside to help poor students acquire the uniforms. For families that have financial or religious reasons not to buy uniforms, many schools have an opt-out policy. This allows for exemptions or waivers from the policy.

Some school principals caution, "You can't have it both ways. [The opt-out policy] created a real disaster."[3] Principal Patrick McDougall said that parents undermined the uniform program at his junior high. As a Christmas present, some parents gave their children permission to avoid the uniform policy. "That's not exactly what we were hoping for," said the frustrated principal.[4] In Garden Grove, California, the uniform program was voluntary. As the year wore on, the number of students wearing uniforms dwindled to less than 30 percent. One eleven-year-old girl explained why she stopped wearing hers: "No one else was wearing them. Kids called me a uniform jerk."[5]

It is important to make certain that the uniforms selected are affordable, easy to care for, and available from several stores. But at the same time, the number of choices provided should be limited. One uniform manufacturer points out that if the purpose of a school uniform is to equalize students, there should not be twenty possible variations. Few students may be able to afford all the possible combinations, and clothing competition will persist.[6]

One way to make a uniform policy successful is to involve students and parents in discussions early on to ensure their support. Surveys can be conducted before school uniform policies are announced, to ensure maximum cooperation. Parents and students can also aid in the selection of the style and colors. After visiting school systems with successful uniform programs, President Clinton noted that "kids liked it better when they adopted their own uniforms of their own choosing."[7] Part of the success of school uniforms in Long Beach,

California, was due to the fact that each school selected its own uniform and that uniforms were made available at almost fifty stores. Fewer than one percent of families asked for a waiver.

It may also make more sense to create dress codes at the school level rather than districtwide. For example, while a certain style, color, or emblem may be associated with gangs in one community, it may not be the case in other towns. Community standards of modesty also vary from area to area.

If a school is going to mandate dress codes or uniforms for students, perhaps teachers and administrators should also be required to follow the policies. Twelve-year-old Lucía Stavig said, "What really gets me mad is when teachers wear many of the same things that are prohibited for students. Why should they get to do that? Just because they're 30 years older than we are?"[8]

A spokesperson for the Council of the Great City Schools was tentative about the effectiveness of uniforms. "From our experience," he said, "I think that uniforms tend to be a positive influence, but whether they are a quick and easy cure for every problem that faces a school district, I think not."[9]

In the end, dress codes and uniforms cannot by themselves solve the complex problems facing the nation's schools. While dress codes and uniforms might result in school improvements, ultimately educators, parents, and students will still have to address larger issues. As two school safety experts put it, "Instituting a dress code alone will not solve the problem of violence in the schools; it is only part of the solution."[10]

**American Civil Liberties Union
Freedom Network**
<http://www.aclu.org/index.html>

**"School Uniforms"
PBS Online News Hour**
<http://www.pbs.org/newshour/infocus/fashion/
school.html>

**U.S. Department of Education and
U.S. Department of Justice**
Manual on School Uniforms
Washington, D.C., 1996
ERIC Document Reproduction Service
No. ED 387 947
<http://www.ed.gov/updates/uniforms.html>

Chapter 1. The Controversy

1. *Ten Critical Threats to America's Children: Warning Signs for the Next Millennium* (Alexandria, Va.: NSBA, 1999).

2. Gayle Hanson, "Kids Choose Dress Blues?" *Insight on the News*, August 26, 1996, p. 42.

3. Jennifer C. as quoted in *Teen*, August 1997, p. 88.

4. National Association of Elementary School Principals, as quoted in John Marks, "Uniform Disagreement," *U.S. News & World Report*, October 26, 1998, p. 30.

5. Susan Byrnes, "Uniforms Gain Popularity at Public School," *Los Angeles Times*, April 12, 1994, p. 3B.

6. John Ritter, "Uniforms Changing Culture of Nation's Classrooms," *USA Today*, October 14, 1998, p. 1A.

7. "Will Changing Dress Codes of Students Help Curb Crimes?" *Jet*, May 11, 1992, p. 16.

8. Ronald D. Stephens, as quoted in Jessica Portner, "California District Points to Uniforms," *Education Week on the Web*, January 21, 1998.

9. "Worth the Risk," *The Indianapolis Star*, March 22, 1996, p. A10.

10. "Should Schools Adopt Dress Codes?" *Current Events*, September 19, 1994, p. 3.

11. "Parents Prompt Pupils to Defy Dress Code," *St. Pete Times*, July 20, 1999, p. 5B.

12. "School Uniforms Cause Dissent," *ACLU Press Release*, May 17, 1997, p. 1.

13. John Marks, "Uniform Disagreement," *U.S. News & World Report*, October 26, 1998, p. 30.

14. Brian Weber, "Schools Eye Dress Code—For Teachers," *Rocky Mountain News*, December 28, 1998, p. 4A.

Chapter 2. The Case for School Dress Codes

1. Peter Blauner, "The Ties that Free," *New York*, December 24–31, 1990, p. 85.

2. Phyllis Parker, as quoted in Valli Herman, "By the Book," *Dallas Morning News*, August 5, 1998, p. 1F.

3. Ronald D. Stephens, *The Art of Safe School Planning*, n.d., <http://www.nssc1.org/home.htm> (February 9, 2000).

4. Erin K. Gauthier, "Feedback," *Milwaukee Journal Sentinel*, November 29, 1998.

5. "Should Schools Adopt Dress Codes?" *Current Events*, September 19, 1994, p. 3.

6. Amy Herdy, "Signs of Trouble," *St. Petersburg Times*, February 22, 1998, p. 1A.

7. Gayle Hanson, "Kids Choose Dress Blues?" *Insight on the News*, August 26, 1996, p. 42.

8. "Will Changing Dress Codes of Students Help Curb Crimes?" *Jet*, May 11, 1992, p. 20.

9. Valli Herman, "By the Book," *Dallas Morning News*, August 5, 1998, p. 1F.

10. John Ritter, "Uniforms Changing Culture of Nation's Classrooms," *USA Today*, October 14, 1998, p. 1A.

11. Brian Weber, "Schools Eye Dress Code—For Teachers," *Rocky Mountain News*, December 28, 1998, p. 4A.

12. Jake, as quoted in <www.razzberry.com/dresscode> (April 20, 1999).

Chapter 3. The Case Against School Dress Codes

1. Herbert Buchsbaum, "The Case of the Gold-Stud Earring," *Scholastic Update*, November 3, 1995, p. 10.

2. Rebecca Rodriguez, "200 March Out of Bastrop High Over Dress Codes," *Fox News Service*, September 3, 1998.

3. "Should Schools Adopt Dress Codes?" *Current Events*, September 19, 1994, p. 3.

4. "California Honor Student Banned from Graduation," *Jet*, July 17, 1995, p. 32.

5. Shelby Oppel, "Third-grader's Braided Hair Sparks Cultural Dispute," *St. Petersburg Times*, December 9, 1996, p. 1B.

6. Jon Bigness, "Valedictorian Sits Out Rite After Clothes Call," *Chicago Tribune*, June 12, 1998, p. 1WC.

7. Tom Kenworthy, "Court Backs School Ban on Grads' African Sashes," *Chicago Sun-Times*, May 24, 1998, p. 22.

8. Steve Jones, "T-shirt Walkout Sends 9 Home," *Fayetteville Observer-Times*, September 30, 1997.

9. Kelly Bietka, "Code Breaking," *Kansas City Star*, October 16, 1998, p. E10.

10. Rick Pierce, "Colorado Killings Lead Area Schools to Consider Banning Trench Coats," *St. Louis Post-Dispatch*, April 28, 1999, p. A1.

11. Sharmaine Lewis, "The School Uniform Debate Continues," *New York Amsterdam News*, June 17, 1998, p. 22.

12. "Should Schools Adopt Dress Codes?" *Current Events*, September 19, 1994, p. 3.

13. Jessica Portner, "Schools Ratchet Up the Rules," *Education Week on the Web*, May 12, 1999.

14. "Schools Tightening Their Dress Codes," *Montreal Gazette*, April 30, 1999, p. B4.

15. Shaun Winfrey, "Who Am I," n.d., <http://cctr.umkc.edu/wicc/real.html> (April 30, 1996).

Chapter 4. The Case for School Uniforms

1. Tamar Lewin, "Public Schools Learning to Like a Uniform Look," *Plain Dealer*, September 27, 1997, p. 2A.

2. Kenneth Cole, "School Uniforms," *Detroit News*, February 24, 1997, p. C1.

3. "Worth the Risk," *The Indianapolis Star*, March 22, 1996, p. A10.

4. Loretta Grantham, "Dress Rehearsal," *Palm Beach Post*, August 24, 1992, p. 5D.

5. William J. Clinton, "Memorandum for the Secretary of Education," Office of the Press Secretary, February 23, 1996.

6. Andrea Atkins and Jeremy Schlosberg, "Dressed to Learn," *Better Homes and Gardens*, August 1996, p. 42.

7. Philomina Harshaw, as quoted in *Manual on School Uniforms* (Washington, D.C.: U.S. Department of Education and U.S. Department of Justice, ERIC Document Reproduction Service No. ED 387 947), 1996.

8. Lewin, p. 2A.

9. Rudy Giuliani, "School Uniforms Foster Pride Among Students," *Filipino Reporter*, April 2, 1998, p. 22.

10. James D. King, "Uniforms as a Safety Measure," *American School & University*, February 1996, p. 38.

11. Don Aucoin, "Weld Pushes for Uniforms in Schools," *Boston Globe*, February 12, 1997, p. A1.

12. Grantham, p. 1D.

13. Veda Morgan, "The Debate Over Dress Code," *The Courier-Journal*, March 4, 1999, p. 1A.

14. John Ritter, "Uniforms Changing Culture of Nation's Classrooms," *USA Today*, October 14, 1998, p. 1A.

15. Deb Levine, "The Ultimate Dress Code," *React*, October 19–25, 1998, p. 5.

16. Cole, p. C1.

17. "Growing Up in Uniform Style," *Fort Worth Star-Telegram*, February 18, 1997, p. 9.

18. Grantham, p. 5D.

19. Levine, p. 5.

20. Ritter, p. 1A.

21. Paul Bedard, "All Uniformly in Agreement," *Insight on the News*, March 25, 1996, p. 37.

22. R.M., as quoted in *Teen*, August 1997, p. 88.

23. "Strict Uniform Policy Elicits Mixed Reaction," *St. Pete Times*, May 13, 1999, p. 3B.

Chapter 5. The Case Against School Uniforms

1. Deb Levine, "The Ultimate Dress Code," *React*, October 19–25, 1998, p. 5.

2. Sybil Renick, "Dressed to Express," n.d., <http://cctr.umkc.edu/wicc/sybil.html> (April 30, 1996).

3. Paul Kandarian, "Schools Mixed on Whether Pupils Should Dress Alike," *The Boston Globe*, April 4, 1999, p. 1.

4. Darla Carter, "Central Students Protest Dress Code," *The Courier-Journal*, March 9, 1999, p. 3B.

5. Kenneth T. Walsh, "Kinderpolitics," *U.S. News & World Report*, September 16, 1996, p. 51.

6. Sharmaine Lewis, "The School Uniform Debate Continues," *New York Amsterdam News*, June 17, 1998, p. 22.

7. Tamar Lewin, "Public Schools Learning to Like a Uniform Look," *Plain Dealer*, September 27, 1997, p. 2A.

8. Jan Ferris, "Schools Rely on a Uniform Trend," *Sacramento Bee*, May 27, 1997, p. A1.

9. Veda Morgan, "The Debate Over Dress Code," *The Courier-Journal*, March 4, 1999, p. 1A.

10. "Are School Uniforms a Good Idea?" *Current Events*, September 18, 1995, p. 3.

11. Mary Shedden, "A Lesson in Fashion," *Gainesville Sun*, March 17, 1996.

12. Families Plus, "Adolescents and Clothes," n.d., <http://www.parenting-qa.com> (February 8, 2000).

13. Kelly Bietka, "Code Breaking," *Kansas City Star*, October 16, 1998, p. E10.

14. Jim Ostroff, "School Dress Code Call Gets Mostly Positive Reactions," *Daily News Record*, February 27, 1996, p. 3.

15. Andrea Atkins and Jeremy Schlosberg, "Dressed to Learn," *Better Homes and Gardens*, August 1996, p. 42.

16. Jessica Portner, "Uniforms Get Credit for Decrease in Discipline Problems," *Education Week on the Web*, February 14, 1996.

17. Cathe Hutchens, "Hasn't Seen the Benefits," *Courier-Journal*, December 14, 1998, p. 8A.

18. Paul Kandarian, "Schools Mixed on Whether Pupils Should Dress Alike," *The Boston Globe*, April 4, 1999, p. 1.

19. Loren Siegel, "Point of View: School Uniforms," *ACLU in Congress on the Web*, March 1, 1996.

Chapter 6. The Bottom Line

1. Rick Pierce, "Colorado Killings Lead Area Schools to Consider Banning Trench Coats," *St. Louis Post-Dispatch*, April 28, 1999, p. A1.

2. Betty Reid, "Central High Takes Steps to Ease T-Shirt Ban," *The Arizona Republic*, September 23, 1998, p. 1.

3. "Strict Uniform Policy Elicits Mixed Reaction," *St. Pete Times*, May 13, 1999, p. 3B.

4. Jan Ferris, "Schools Rely on a Uniform Trend," *Sacramento Bee*, May 27, 1997, p. A1.

5. Gayle Hanson, "Kids Choose Dress Blues?" *Insight on the News*, August 26, 1996, p. 42.

6. Laura McEvoy, as quoted in Lisa Levenson, "Uniform Looks," *Dallas Morning News*, February 11, 1997, p. 26A.

7. "Transcript of Clinton Remarks to Community of Augusta State University," February 5, 1997, Augusta, Georgia.

8. Personal interview with Lucía Stavig, May 23, 1999.

9. Henry Duval, as quoted in Jessica Portner, "California District Points to Uniforms," *Education Week on the Web*, January 21, 1998.

10. Beverly H. Johns and John P. Keenan, *Techniques for Managing a Safe School* (Denver, Colo.: Love Publishing, 1997), p. 69.

Barbour, Scott. *Teen Violence*. San Diego: Greenhaven Press, 1999.

Farish, Leah. *The First Amendment: Freedom of Speech, Religion, and the Press*. Berkeley Heights, NJ: Enslow Publishers, 1998.

Jahn, Karon L. *School Dress Codes v. The First Amendment: Ganging Up on Student Attire* (October, 1992). ERIC Document Reproduction Service ED 355595.

McEldowney, Jane, et. al. *Piecing It Together: A Guide to Academic Success*. New York: Prentice Hall, 1998.

Miller, Maryann. *Coping With Weapons and Violence in School and on Your Streets*. New York: Rosen Publishing Group, 1999.

Rubinstein, Ruth P. *Dress Codes: Meanings and Messages in American Culture*. Boulder, Colo.: Westview Press, 1995.

Trespacz, Karen L. *Ferrell v. Dallas I.S.D.: Hairstyles in Schools*. Berkeley Heights, NJ: Enslow Publishers, 1998.

Wolff, Lisa. *Gangs*. San Diego: Lucent Books, 2000.

Further Reading

Index